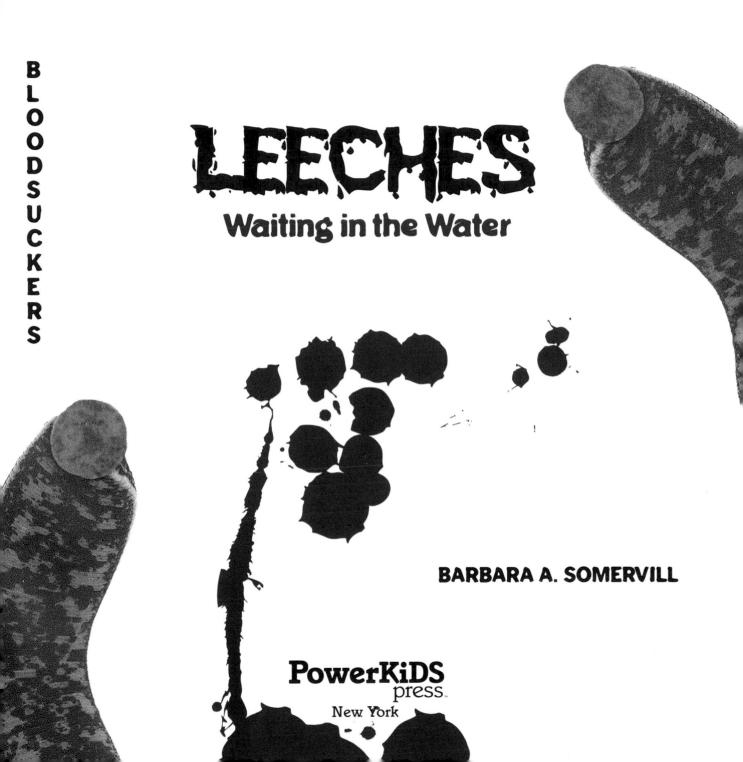

BLOODSUCKERS

LEECHES
Waiting in the Water

BARBARA A. SOMERVILL

PowerKiDS press.
New York

Published in 2008 by The Rosen Publishing Group, Inc.
29 East 21st Street, New York, NY 10010

First Edition

Editors: Joanne Randolph and Geeta Sobha
Book Design: Dean Galiano
Layout Design: Greg Tucker
Photo Researcher: Nicole Pristash

Photo Credits: Cover, p. 19 © Frank Greenaway/Getty Images; pp. 5, 9, 11, 15, 17 © Shutterstock.com; p. 7 © Robert Maier/Animals Animals; p. 13 © www.istockphoto.com/Grace Tan; p. 21 © C. C. Lockwood/Animals Animals.

Library of Congress Cataloging-in-Publication Data

Somervill, Barbara A.
    Leeches : waiting in the water / Barbara A. Somervill. — 1st ed.
        p. cm. — (Bloodsuckers)
    Includes index.
    ISBN-13: 978-1-4042-3801-5 (library binding)
    ISBN-10: 1-4042-3801-8 (library binding)
    1. Leeches—Juvenile literature. I. Title.
    QL391.A6S65 2008
    592'.66—dc22
                                              2006103425

Manufactured in the United States of America

CONTENTS

MEET THE LEECH

On a field trip to a pond, the teacher points out duckweed, pond lilies, cattails, and reeds. Wind blows one student's ball cap into the pond. He takes off his shoes and goes in to get the hat. He has returned with more than just his hat, though.

In those few seconds, a leech had firmly fixed itself to his leg. He did not feel a thing! The teacher slides her finger under the leech's head, removes it, and cleans the bite spot with **antiseptic**. The class had gone to the pond to learn about plants. They had not planned to learn about the bloodsucking leech!

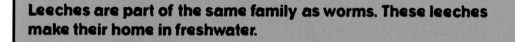

Leeches are part of the same family as worms. These leeches make their home in freshwater.

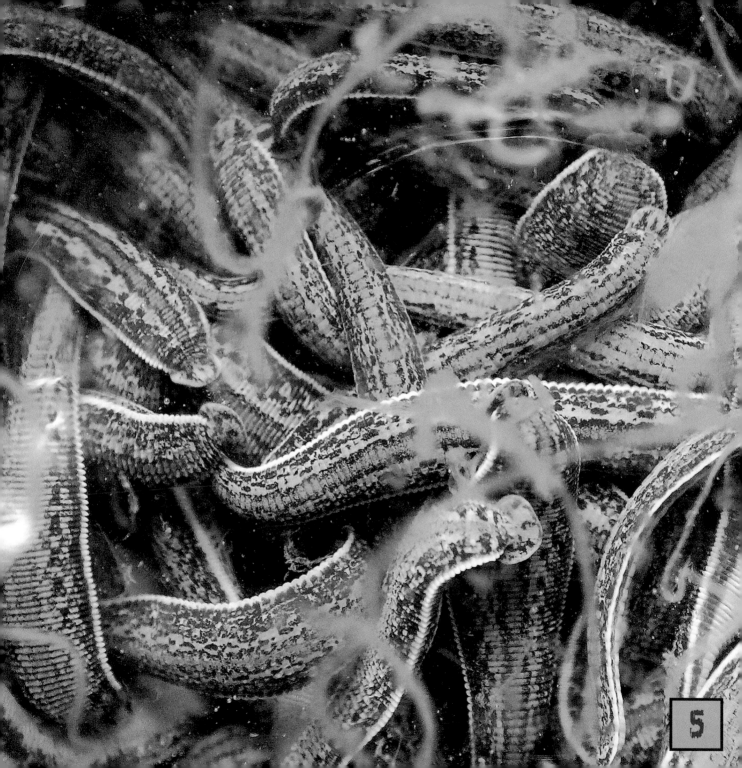

THREE KINDS OF LEECHES

All leeches fall into one of three basic groups. Jawed leeches have many sharp teeth that they use to bite into their **prey**. They suck blood from an animal for food.

Jawless leeches have a **proboscis**. The proboscis is a thin, sharp tube that slides into the animal. This allows the leech to suck blood.

Worm leeches do not drink blood at all. They have no jaws or teeth. They have a large mouth and eat their prey whole. Worm leeches usually eat small worms, snails, and bugs.

The flat round part at each end of this freshwater leech is called a sucker. The mouth is part of the front sucker.

7

A PARASITE TO BEHOLD

There are about 500 different **species** of leeches. Worm leeches are **predators**. They kill and eat their prey. Jawed and jawless leeches are **parasites**. A parasite feeds off an animal but does not usually kill the animal.

Most leeches look like flat, wide worms. This is to be expected since the leech's closest kin is the earthworm. Leeches can be from ½ to 8 inches (1–20 cm) in size. They can be brown, black, green, or red. Some leeches have stripes or spots. All leeches have 34 **segments** in their body.

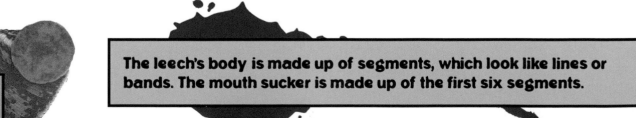

The leech's body is made up of segments, which look like lines or bands. The mouth sucker is made up of the first six segments.

WATERY HOMES

Leeches live in very still, quiet bodies of freshwater, like ponds, small lakes, or slow-moving rivers. There are a few leeches that live in salt water.

Land leeches like wet rain forests. They can be found in low bushes or damp, rotting leaves. Some live in regular forests, near fresh springs or muddy ground.

Some leeches stay close to where they lay their eggs. They will feed their young and keep them safe from predators.

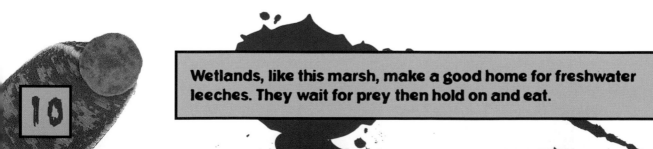

Wetlands, like this marsh, make a good home for freshwater leeches. They wait for prey then hold on and eat.

TIME TO EAT

Leeches will feed on turtles, fish, ducks, or water snakes. Some leeches wait for animals to drink at a pond. When the animal steps into the water, the leech bites and feeds until it is full.

When a bloodsucking leech bites, three things happen. The leech oozes a gluey matter around the bite so it sticks better to the animal. Leeches add a painkiller into the wound, so the animal feels nothing. The leech also adds something to keep the blood from thickening. Once full, the leech drops off the animal. It may not need to feed again for months.

This leech has eaten its fill of blood and has dropped off the person. The leech will then digest, or break down, the blood.

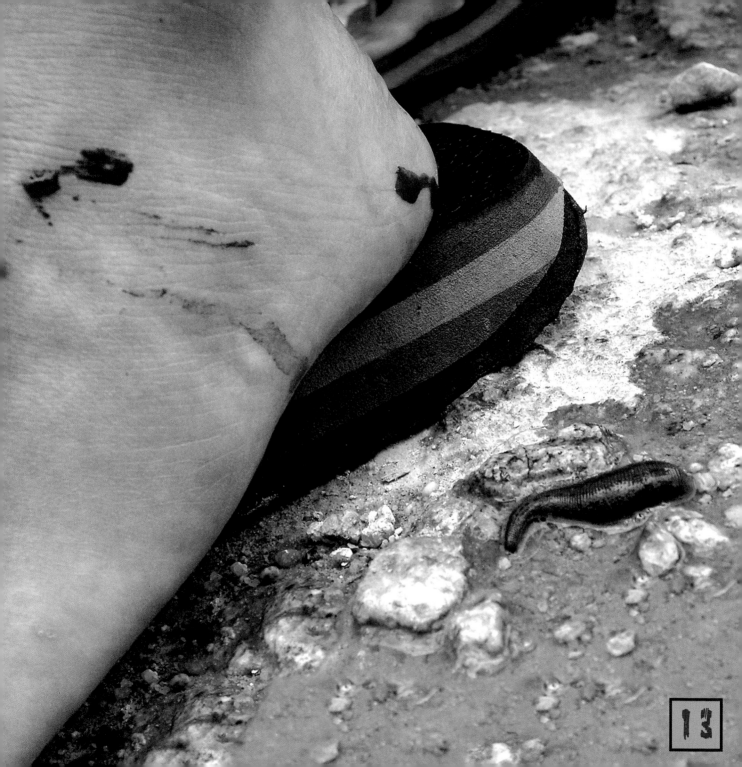

13

WAITING FOR BLOOD

Leeches wait for their prey to come along. When they are hungry, leeches notice light and movement easily. They search the area around them by moving their head. They reach out with their body and then remain still.

When the prey gets close, the leech crawls forward. It moves much like an inchworm and feels around for the prey. Once they have fed, leeches go to a dark place to digest the blood.

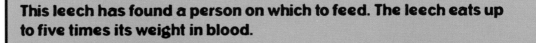

This leech has found a person on which to feed. The leech eats up to five times its weight in blood.

15

TASTY FOOD

A large number of animals feed on leeches. Among the larger fish that eat leeches are largemouth bass, perch, sturgeon, and catfish. Crayfish crawl along river bottoms to hunt for leeches. Beetles and dragonfly **larvae** also like to eat leeches.

Mallard ducks and wood ducks also eat leeches. It is only fair. After all, leeches feed on the ducks, too!

This mallard duck may eat a few leeches as part of its dinner. It may not know it, but it may be giving food to a few leeches, too.

LEECH SENSES

Leeches do not see, smell, or feel in the same way **mammals** do. They can have from 2 to 10 or more eyes. They have no nose. They smell using nerves located on their head. They can sense changes in light, temperature, and motion. They use this information to find prey.

Leeches also breathe differently from mammals. They take in **oxygen** through their skin.

The leech uses special parts at the front of its body to look for and find prey.

A LEECH'S LIFE

Leeches have only two stages in their life cycle. First they are eggs, then they become leeches. All leeches can produce and **fertilize** eggs.

A leech puts out a jellylike foam for a **cocoon**. It places the eggs inside the cocoon. Once dried, the cocoon is hard on the outside. The cocoon is very strong and keeps the eggs from being harmed. After weeks or even months, the eggs open and adult leeches come out.

These adult leeches have fixed themselves to the belly of a snapping turtle for a feast.

THE HEALING LEECH

Most people find leeches gross. However, there is one species of leech that truly helps humans. That leech is the **medicinal** leech. For thousands of years, humans have used those leeches to treat illnesses.

Today, doctors are once more using leeches to help sick people. In an operation to mend burns, a doctor may move skin from one place on a person to another place. Leeches are then applied to the cuts to return blood flow to the area. Leeches are becoming a part of modern medicine.

22

GLOSSARY

antiseptic (an-tee-SEP-tik) Something that is used to keep cuts clean.

cocoon (kuh-KOON) A covering made by some animals to keep their eggs safe.

fertilize (FUR-tuh-lyz) To make eggs that can turn into young.

larvae (LAHR-vee) Animals in the early life stage in which they have a wormlike form.

mammals (MA-mulz) Warm-blooded animals that have a backbone and hair.

medicinal (meh-DIS-nul) Having to do with medicine.

oxygen (OK-sih-jen) A gas in the air that animals need to breathe.

parasites (PER-uh-syts) Living things that live in, on, or with another living thing.

predators (PREH-duh-terz) Animals that kill other animals for food.

prey (PRAY) An animal that is hunted by another animal for food.

proboscis (pruh-BAH-sus) The long, tube-shaped mouthpart of an insect.

segments (SEG-ments) Parts of things.

species (SPEE-sheez) One kind of living thing.

INDEX

WEB SITES

Due to the changing nature of Internet links, PowerKids Press has developed an online list of Web sites related to the subject of this book. This site is updated regularly. Please use this link to access the list:
www.powerkidslinks.com/bsu/leeches/